The First BEN WICKS Treasury

"At the risk of appearing facetious, sir, it also gets lonely at the bottom."

The First BEN WICKS Treasury

METHUEN

Toronto   New York   London   Sydney   Auckland

Canadian Cataloguing in Publication Data

Wicks, Ben, 1926–
   The first Ben Wicks treasury

ISBN 0-458-99630-0

1. Canadian wit and humor, Pictorial. I. Title.

NC1449.W53A4 1985   741.5'971   C85-
099138-2

Design / Don Fernley
Cover photo / John Reeves

Printed and bound in Canada

1 2 3 4   85   89 88 87 86

To Doreen

Introduction

I have a background in art.

I mention this to offset all the snide remarks that will come from those who figure that they know something about art.

I went to one of the finest art schools in the world.

The Camberwell School of Art in London, England.

It's true that I only went for two weeks...evening classes...but in that time I did, if you will look closely, manage to pick up many of the finer points needed to become successful as a cartoonist.

How to draw badly and how to work in colour...black and white.

As with most cartoonists, the human form causes me problems.

(Those with filthy minds can keep their remarks to themselves.)

It's one of the most difficult things to draw.

I have overcome many of the problems in this area.

Since I cannot draw feet, I sit most of my people behind a desk.

Hands, the most difficult, are placed in pockets or, in the case of women, behind backs.

Many people will be amazed that a professional cartoonist will confess to such failings.

They are not aware that cartoonists are not alone in being lousy "drawers."

Michelangelo painted only on ceilings. And only those ceilings that
were difficult to see up close. To see Michelangelo's hands and the
problems he had with fingers it's necessary to hire a fire brigade
ladder. Since, as yet, no fire engine has ever been able to make it up
the stairs of the Sistine Chapel, the famous artist's reputation remains
intact.

Turner had problems with feet. Waves and water? Terrific. Feet? No
way. All the people in Turner's pictures are fishermen and are painted
sitting down in boats. Constable? Trees. All his people are drawn and
painted lying on the grass. But standing up? Never! Rembrandt? Head
and shoulders only.

Even the Mona Lisa has her hands crossed and hidden in her lap.

But, and here is the big plus with my drawings, they tell a story. And no
one-line rubbishy titles like "The Hay Cart" or "Sunflower" or
"Laughing Cavellia." Mine are story stories.

The people I draw talk. They don't just sit there with a silly grin on their
face.

So there you have it. A book with people in it that talk and say lots of
intelligent things. Sometimes my pen has slipped and a good-looking
girl has appeared. These drawings have also been included (though I
must be honest, for those of you who like this kind of thing, all are
wearing their clothes).

So there you have it.
A book of talking people.
Famous talking people.
You can actually hear what they are saying.
It's an incredible bargain.
Many of you are asking how I can make money from such a low price.
I don't.
I do it for love.
Love of you, my fellow man and woman.
So enjoy.

Ben Wicks

P.S. Those lousy good-for-nothing loafers who are standing in the store
reading this without paying, put it back and give others who have
money a chance to get at it.

I

This part of the book concerns itself with life in Canada.

Many people will find this section boring.

It is boring.

That's because we're boring.

You, that is.

I mention this to save you time.

If you have a bus to catch or are reading this in a store that is about to close, skip this part and go straight to the next section.

**"An earthquake warning is in effect.
Keep away from tall buildings."**

"Well if it isn't Mr. Trudeau. What brings you to Canada?"

"Come quick, Warden. There's been another mass break-in."

"I blame the unemployed. If they didn't work in the first place they wouldn't be unemployed."

"We should never have told him how dangerous it is out there."

"Remind me again. Am I working or striking today?"

"Good evening. Owing to cutbacks tonight's CBC news will be a repeat of last night's CBC news."

"The only way to create more jobs is to fire a few people!"

"Give me a home, where no buffalo roam, and the oil and the millionaires play..."

"Maybe, with luck, his bags will lose him."

"I'll talk, I'll talk, but don't mention the constitution again."

"You're wasting your time. The Government got there before you."

"I still don't see how dropping a bomb on Alberta and Quebec helps Canada."

"Okay. Which one of you is the politician?"

"You've got the election, Pope, Queen disease. Hide under the bed for a week."

"Cheer up Frank, things could be worse. We could be living on the outside."

"We can loan you money to buy a house but you'll need a house for collateral."

"He's in a meeting."

"You can't expect everyone to like you."

"When did you first experience this craving for getting back to work?"

"Isn't it wonderful, Mother? Fred's gone to work determined to cross the picket line."

"Here's one for us. 'University graduates needed.'"

"It's Sussex Drive. The Chinese foreign secretary is in town."

"What are you, some kind of nut?"

"Congratulations Mr. Thomas, of the 2,000 job applications we've decided to keep yours on file."

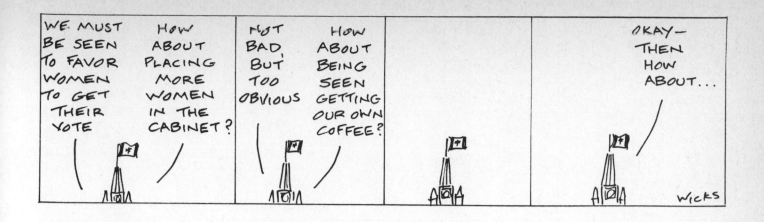

"It was terrible. I dreamt I was giving a speech in the Senate and woke up and found I was."

"When I ask you what you want it for, 'to spend' is hardly the answer I need."

"Frank Evans will not be sending cards this year. Stop. He's too busy sending resumes."

"I'm forced to lay off more staff and I want two volunteers."

"Just because you don't like any of them is no excuse. You've got to vote."

"Should I let him get out of bed to vote, even if I don't approve of his political choice?"

"I want to vote for Broadbent but I'm afraid he might win."

"Does this mean we're going to miss the Pope, the Queen or the election?"

"Oh dear, I think John Turner has used a tactile greeting again."

"I don't care who you're voting for, you're paid to clean all the offices."

"Just for the hell of it, let's say we're voting NDP."

"It must have rained in the night."

"We could protest the cutbacks by going on strike, but who would notice?"

"Sure, I like John Turner, but I like Mila Mulroney better."

"If they ask if they can rejoin the colonies, pretend you haven't heard."

"How we doing?"

"If we're going to beat Turner, I'll have
to be more decisive...I think."

"Remind me again—once I sit down,
what do I shout at the dogs?"

"The Pope isn't running."

"First right, second left, and Manpower
is on your right."

"I'm really for Mulroney but I couldn't find a big enough button."

"Harold just got laid off."

"And you say you had these given to you, is that right?"

"I'm not one to mix religion and politics."

"Are you getting enough to eat, I mean, more than us on the outside?"

"Mr Evans, Harry Thomas. He hasn't got the Order of Canada either."

"I'm unemployed yet you don't see me complaining."

"Isn't it exciting? He's the first leadership candidate who's taken an oath of silence."

"I'm sorry, Mr. Evans. The answer is still 'no.'"

"Excuse me, sir. It's customary to shake the hand of royalty."

"It's been brought to our attention that you still have a shirt on your back."

"I can change it to Mulroney but you'll need a fatter arm."

"Gee, what do you know. Mila wears the same size dress that I do."

"The doctor says you must rest easy and that I must not tell you that you've been laid off."

"Just because you're new doesn't mean those nasty Liberals can shout at you. Shout right back."

"In order to create more jobs I have decided to fire the following."

41

"I'll be honest. Getting approval for your loan will not be easy seeing that you need the money."

"Madam Speaker, I accuse the Government of frivolous behaviour toward a leaderless Opposition."

"Just because they have the same initials hardly seems a suitable reason for me to support Jean Chrétien."

"I know I said the dollar was shrinking but making them bigger doesn't help."

"Okay, what's it going to be, your way or ours?"

"Vote for me and I'll cut the crime rate."

"How many days to the next recess?"

"Then he, the boss, said 'How would you like to save the company $1,500 a month?'"

"Plus, our candidate has two great new ideas. He's going to work hard and be an honest politician."

"Okay, okay. So we're a bit late getting this letter to you."

"He needs cheering up. Lie to him about the economy."

"I plan on paying you back out of my lottery winnings."

"The silver bells and cockle shells are exempt but the pretty maids all in a row do not qualify."

"What you need is plenty of fresh air and exercise."

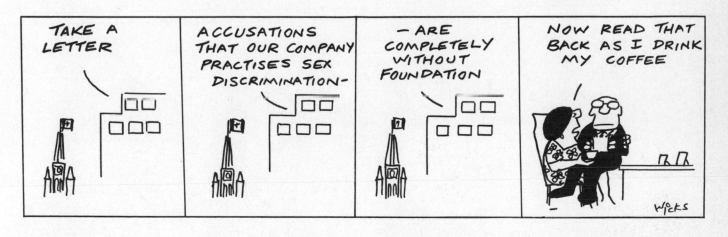

47

"Do you have anything other than a wife, three children and a dog to offer as collateral?"

"We interrupt this news to bring you even worse news."

"Would monkey food be a legitimate business expense?"

"What happened to the lion tamer job we sent you to yesterday?"

II

For those of you who have never travelled and have no wish to find out
  how the "other half lives," this section is not for you.
Most of the people who are anybody will be nobodies to you.
What they have done or are doing will be of no concern since you feel
  it's doubtful that you'll ever meet any of them.
At least not in this life.
Try sport, or the movies.
You sound like the kind of person that would be interested in these.

**"We don't have an aisle seat but we do
have three middle seats behind each
other."**

"We're closing the gap, Sir. Just 3 rifles, 2 helmets and a pair of army socks and we've caught up."

"I don't think it was wise to end your remarks to Haig with 'You're the boss.'"

"What's Lady Di really like?"

"Let me through, I'm an economist."

"Great news. The economy is turning around."

"The people of Afghanistan have run out of bouquets of flowers...over."

"Yeah, this is my first time. How did you know?"

"Contact mission control. We have a problem."

"And you say it will definitely protect me
in the event of a star war?"

"All those who feel I should continue as
chairman signify by saying 'Beep.'"

"If you don't stop complaining about
overcrowding, Evans, you'll be taken out
of solitary."

"Next wicket, please."

"Who do I see about doing business with China?"

"You mean you change every four years?"

"He says he's here seeking support for Zanuk Zuk of Pluto for President of the Universe."

"Can he call you back? He's waiting for things to bottom out."

"Sure they're good. They're the same ones we sell to your opponents."

"If you're going to ask for money, do like I do, ask for a billion."

"And I figure if I can get the organized torturers' vote, I can win the election."

"We consider money to support your campaign for President would be a bad risk."

"My old granny used to say, 'It's no good crying over spilt milk.'"

"And now, for all you fight fans..."

"What do you mean 'I, of all people, should support hunger strikes'?"

"There's only one boss up here and he says you can't take it with you."

"I have bad news for you, P.Q.8. We're taking on a P.Q.9."

"Let's throw a little scare into white man. Make the next one a mushroom cloud."

"What we need is a new weapon to destroy the new weapon that they will use to destroy our new weapon."

"Cut back on the peace marches."

"We're waiting for the big bang."

"The one who walked on the moon ain't running."

"Funny how the Druze, Christians and Lebanese all look alike from up here."

"Oh, General, how silly of me. I didn't mean that all cruise missiles are terrible things."

"Earth to Pluto. No sign of intelligent life. Over and out."

"I've done it! A hydrogen bomb that will fit in a bread box."

"Inform the American advisers that I wish to speak to them again."

"But Mr. Reagan, if my death squads stop killing, what will we call them?"

"Wouldn't you know it. I'm allergic to fish."

"I'm against the nuclear build-up—on the other hand..."

"The computer wants a four day week."

"Do you have an appointment?"

"I'm afraid you have the wrong number...however..."

"Before we vote on this motion let me remind you again as to where I stand."

"Wow, General. You're really dressed to kill."

"We're ready when you are with the transplant."

"What's wrong with being unemployed?
We are and I don't mind."

"Brother, can you spare a dollar?"

"Remember, Harold. That's the President
of the United States on there."

"Have you tried Saturn or Mercury?"

"Boy, what a day. The boss got laid off by the union."

"The warden wants you to go on a hunger strike, Mulrooney."

"It's our newest model. It'll tell you which computer you should have bought instead."

"If crime doesn't pay, how come he can afford an expensive lawyer?"

"I think it's our arms negotiator—he's crying."

"We've decided to make the company more efficient and we'd like you to help—by leaving."

"I think I've tapped in to the Pentagon."

"Miss Jones. Check around and find out if we're the only ones who haven't been laid off."

"I'm not here at the moment. However, if you would like to leave your prayer..."

"Oh look, dear. An English one."

"These expense claims of yours are coming down, Evans. It's time you stepped aside for a younger man."

"Put me down for Ferraro and Reagan."

"The last thing I remember was being told that star wars would mean more jobs."

"I've got a great idea. Just for the hell of it, let's agree on something."

"He's just stepped out. Would you like to leave a last message?"

"How do I know it's a real nuclear bomb?"

"Do you have change of a 50?"

"Who would you like to see win the next election—Cluka, the wise, or Tama, the great?"

"They've reached an agreement. They're going to stop now and come back after lunch."

"And if the union asks you 'what's the bottom line?', tell them that it's something we just hit."

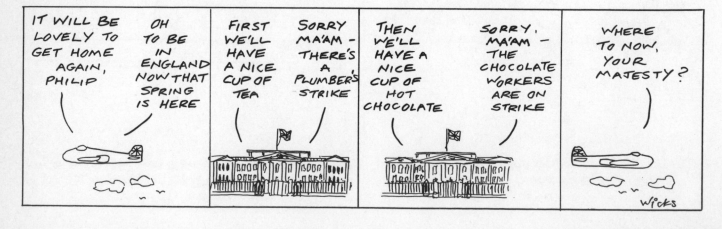

"Just because they're having silly old talks doesn't mean there'll be no more wars."

"Sure he quit when the going got tough, but is that any reason not to vote for him in the next election?"

"The idea is that we give them to the Russians as a good will gesture."

"In keeping with modern trends, I have decided to appoint a vice-devil."

"Star War and arms talks? First left, second right—you can't miss them."

"It says here that things are going to get worse before they get better."

"Sure I think we should keep Sakharov here...which one is he?"

"And while it's true that our Lord never had to concern himself with an election..."

"Mine is taken."

"We've come from a planet with an
overpopulation problem."

"Of course it's unethical. It's business."

"And if we meet any Americans, all
saucers will form a circle."

"So the last arms batch was faulty, quit worrying. The Israeli order was from the same batch."

"We will never be the first to use the bomb, unless, of course, we're 'chickened' into it."

"The economy turned around just before it got to me."

"We're ready with the launching of your secret space shot, sir."

"Watch the one with the pole."

"Then this guy, Reagan, says let's talk about banning weapons in space."

"Hey there, your Holiness. I'm allowed visitors."

"I'd like to withdraw the money I deposited for a rainy day."

"Someone is giving off peace vibes and I want that person to stop."

"Your request for a million dollars to 'set-up shop' in South America has been rejected."

"Surely there must be someone we can try our new weapons on."

"Yours is the clear voice of reason, Evans. Cool it!"

"Don't blame me. The computer says you still owe money."

"Maybe it's time we called for an economic summit."

"Should I tell him that they're holding his job open for him at the atomic plant?"

"Damn it Jim, the world's gone crazy. No one wants a war anymore."

"How badly do you want the loan?"

"They said there were guerillas in the area but this is ridiculous."

"It's true your overdraft is not the size of Argentina's. However..."

"I call it a union and here's how it works. You pay me dues..."

"The men are unhappy. They've found out that you're making almost as much money as they are."

"In keeping with the times, we're cutting back on costs, your Majesty."

"My cellmate wants to hang mistletoe."

"I saw him first."

YOU TOLD AMNESTY INTERNATIONAL THAT PEOPLE IN CHILE ARE BEING TORTURED

— IF YOU DON'T TELL US WHY YOU LIED —

— YOU'LL BE TORTURED AGAIN

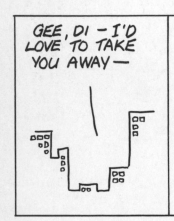
GEE, DI — I'D LOVE TO TAKE YOU AWAY —

— FROM THE HUMDRUM, BORING, DAILY GRIND —

— OF ROYAL DUTIES THAT YOU'RE FORCED TO PERFORM —

— BUT WHAT ABOUT CHARLES?

HOW MANY TIMES MUST I TELL YOU —

— NO SMOKING INSIDE THE HORSE

YOU DON'T WANT THE CRUISE MISSILE?

AND I SUPPOSE YOU'D RATHER LIVE IN PEACE —

— THAN BE BURNT TO A CRISP —

— FIGHTING FOR WHAT I BELIEVE IN

"This is not a picture of Mars. This is a photo of Lebanon."

"Good grief, you're right. It is a space ship."

"Mr. Lee Iacocca ain't gonna like this."

"First, I'm going to wipe out poverty."

III

You don't like sport?
Of course you like sport.
Everyone likes sport.
Even those who are hopeless in sport, like sport.
So you never came first.
Without you there would be no first.
The first can't be first if no one else shows up.
The fact that you showed up was the reason that whoever found
    themselves in front of you came first.
So quit worrying.
You were never last.
You were always second.
Now read on and shut up.

You want to get away from it all.
Of course you do.
We all do.
Then sit back and watch the magic moments brought back.
The wonderful way you were treated at the airport.
The terrific travel agency that booked you on all those wonderful trips.
The glorious times you had waiting for your luggage.
That lovely cab driver you met who tried so hard to find your hotel.
You've changed your mind?
You don't want to travel?
Then skip to the next section. Especially if you're single.
You're not single? Okay okay...Just do as you're told....

"If the Russians don't enter the Olympics,
does that mean our runners won't need
to run so fast?"

"You're boring, inarticulate and dull.
The talk shows will love you."

"It wasn't made to be good, it was made
as a tax shelter."

"Of course you're not interrupting
anything. Come on in."

"Pull over."

"Guess what? They had a January sale at the zoo."

"Don't you want to watch the Actra Awards before you leave?"

"Here's one from a J.R. He wants Dallas, Texas."

"You're playing too many video games."

"I know who shot J.R."

"It's tragic really. It was his first day of jogging on his lunch hour and he got hit by a bus."

"FIRE!"

"Business or pleasure?"

"You drank too much over Christmas."

"Can you be a little more specific than
'anywhere not run by a bunch of
clowns'?"

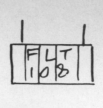

"That flight has been cancelled. Would you like to go somewhere else?"

"I didn't know the Pope was on our plane."

"How much is it without the cart?"

"Who said anything about two seats?"

"Sure I'm interested in your party. Shall we bring food?"

"How come you never smile like that?"

"And don't buy me a Michael Jackson ticket for my birthday. I can't afford it."

"Who do I see about a refund?"

"When I said it's a widebody I was speaking about the aircraft."

"When I asked if you'd considered politics, I was speaking to the dummy."

"She's watching the soaps."

"Did you notice how content Gandhi was with just one cheap piece of clothing?"

"I told him he couldn't take it with him but he wouldn't listen."

"How can you be sure that the Iranians won't mistake us for an oil tanker?"

"Stop thinking about the office and enjoy the holiday."

"Look at it this way. All the movies you didn't want to see are brought right into your own home."

"...so, sick of the jungle, you decide to leave Tarzan and go into politics."

"When they lift their ban on the Olympics, I'll lift my ban on their desks."

"I'm sure your husband is in terrific shape but by 'trade in' we mean a car."

"Immigration? Second on the right."

"I think we picked up the wrong suitcase."

"It's new. We use strangers and call it a no-name product."

"It's still not loud enough."

"One resolution down, 5 to go."

"And now, for the best singers in a 5,000 voice choir or over..."

"It's your own fault. I told you not to get Pay TV."

"If you don't like the music, why are you watching the awards?"

"Excuse me. I don't wish to pry but who's up front?"

"Oh yeah! Well I'll tell you something. If you were half the man Gretzky is..."

"I told you we wouldn't need them, but you wouldn't listen."

"So far, so good. Now to find you a job."

"This one I found inside that one."

"Okay, you can go on a Terry Fox Run but remember, no running."

"Sure I'm thrilled I got nominated for an Oscar but are you sure you've got the right Paul Newman?"

"The patients have rebelled and are eating everything in sight."

"That one was from Mary Kay, that one from Fuller Brush and that one was a census taker."

"Now which of last year's resolutions would you like a crack at this year?"

"The word I hear is that they're fast becoming an endangered species."

"It's your own fault. You should have paid Dr. Frankenstein the user fees he asked for."

"Look, if you don't like tobacco you can always quit."

"Wake up Chimo. You forgot to unplug the video game."

"You can come out Frank. I know you've broken your quit smoking resolution."

"He must have been a heavy smoker. There's an ashtray in here."

"He had four legs, a tail and a patch over one eye."

"How long is it since you gave up smoking?"

"How come when I booked during the seat sale no one mentioned standing?"

"Are they low in tar content?"

"Your seat to Denver has been taken,
however we do have one to Hong Kong."

"Smoking, non-smoking or trying to
quit?"

"Sorry. Coke, Pepsi, 7UP, Perrier or
Sprite, but no water."

"There's a man outside with Hitler's
diaries that include last week's entries."

Panel 1: THERE GOES A TORONTO ARGO PLAYER

FLIGHT

Panel 2: HOW DO YOU KNOW?

Panel 3: HE KEEPS DROPPING HIS LUGGAGE

Panel 4: HA HO HE HA HO

WICKS

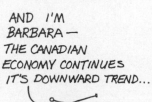

Panel 1: HELLO, I'M BARBARA... AND I'M MARY LOU

Panel 2: AND I'M BARBARA— THE CANADIAN ECONOMY CONTINUES IT'S DOWNWARD TREND...

Panel 3: DESPITE THIS SETBACK SIGNS OF A TURN-AROUND ARE BEGINNING TO APPEAR

Panel 4: THIS IS BARBARA LOU — GOODNIGHT

Wicki

Panel 1: WHO DO YOU THINK WILL WIN THE OSCAR FOR BEST ACTOR? WHO'S BEEN NOMINATED?

Panel 2: PAUL NEWMAN AND A GUY CALLED GANDHI WHO'S HE?

Panel 3: A LITTLE SKINNY GUY WITH STEEL RIMMED GLASSES

WICKS

Panel 4: PAUL NEWMAN!

Panel 1: COME QUICK, MAVIS—

Panel 2: I THINK IT'S SOMETHING SERIOUS

Panel 3: KNOWLTON NASH IS CRYING

WICKS

"So steroids have a side effect. Look at the bright side. Now you can really run faster."

"If you read our 'bargain flight' ad carefully you'll see no one said anything about a seat."

"Okay, you were at the ball game and you started to shout. Then what?"

"So we got the last two cheap seats. Now what?"

"And now the best Canadian actor in an unseen, unknown, unheard of series is..."

"Can I call you back? Linda Evans is about to thump Joan Collins."

"Inflation is 1%, interest rates are 3% and Farrah Fawcett is prime minister."

"Of course we've seen this before, silly. It's the news."

"I'm sorry to bother you. Do you have any steroids, I'm fresh out."

IMMIGRATION

"Two ballet dancers, one weightlifter and a mixed doubles want in."

"Surely there's another way to get the ghetto vote other than break-dancing lessons?"

"Smoking or non-smoking?"

"For Pete's sake, Harold, give him something."

"If it's the original, how come da Vinci is spelt 'de Vinsi'?"

"My advice to you is to forget show biz, return home and take the girl with you."

IV

For those married readers who have forgotten what it was like to be
   single, this section is for you.
You need reminding that being single is not all that it's cracked up to be.
Just a lot of sex and parties.
And who needs that?
Put your hand down! Everyone in the bookstore is looking at you.

**"Are you aware, Miss Jones, that what
you seek more of is the root of all evil?"**

"Heads, you'll be Vice President, tails,
I'll be President."

"On the contrary. If I didn't like women,
I wouldn't have married one."

"Of course she'll like it. It smells like a
credit card."

"Are you aware that what you are asking
me for is the root of all evil?"

"If you want your money back, say so. Don't give me that 'but he's a priest' stuff."

"Can you keep my daughter in the manner to which she is accustomed?"

"When you say all feminists should be shot, are you including mothers?"

"Just because he lives with you, doesn't make him a dependant."

"John, you must come. We're having all the candidates over for group therapy."

"Dreadful news, sir. We've just found that sex causes tumours in mice."

"But seriously..."

"They have a tortoise-shell frame and are in a brown case."

"Oh yes, sir. That's definitely you."

"They've taken a hostage and are demanding new anti-abortion laws."

"For starters, you can stop believing everything you read in the newspapers."

"I'm putting you on a strict diet. Quit eating and come back and see me in a month."

"How's your typing?"

"You may smoke if you wish."

"I'd like a pound of anything that the
fruit flies overlooked."

"I want the Pope to notice me in a
crowd."

"What I'd like is to talk to Geraldine
Ferraro, man to man."

"What do you mean, you're both male?"

"Sure you have suicidal tendencies, so
stop looking into the future."

"You certainly have a way with
mistletoe."

"What do you mean, it's too much? I haven't told you the price yet."

"Sure I can make you look like Dolly Parton. Now what about your face?"

"Do you see a tall, dark, handsome man taking me away from a short, bald, ugly boss?"

"I'm a sweet sensitive girl and if you don't give me a raise I'll break both your legs."

"Peggy tells me you're in politics."

"Excuse me, sir. The word processor is leaking."

"My advice to you is, get married and then come back and see us."

"Has anyone seen Miss Evans?"

"He's either an Arab prince or a divorce lawyer."

"We the jury find the victim of the rape, guilty, as charged."

"My wife left me and now I can't pay my bills."

"Of course it's a crumby seat. You're sitting in the women's section."

"I'd like something for the woman that needs everything."

"Before you say anything, I've checked with your office."

"Working for us will require you to follow certain guidelines, right Miss Jones?"

"So how goes the battle?"

"The party's off."

"Let me remind you that it's a jungle out there."

"You can't fire me. I quit!"

"Where's the 'willing to take anyone' file? I have a 'willing to do anything.'"

"You mean you haven't got a wife? Then why are you playing around?"

"Good morning. I'm with Guard Dogs Inc."

"Kiss me and I'll become a handsome prince, strongly supportive of equal rights for women."

"Okay then. We'll live together for a while and if it works out, then we'll get married."

"What's with Andrew and Katie Rabett?"

"We're all out of servile models. How about the standard cook and housekeeper?"

"Sure the shoe down the road went for $95,000 but I'm talking boots."

"If Prince Charles phones, tell him I'll call back."

"I had all my eggs in one basket and there was a hole in the basket."

"How do you feel about sexual harassment?"

"Are you trying to tell me that the girl he's living with is his wife?"

"No, sir. I'm not the secretary, I'm the boss. Are you the secretary?"

"When are you having a special on prices?"

"Wow. Are you ever lucky. The computer has matched you with Prince Charles."

"My secretary doesn't understand me."

V

Here's the one section you cannot skip.

For those of you who are not married, read it and find out what it's really like.

For those of you who are married—read it and find out what it's really like.

"You never take me anywhere."

GIFT SUGGESTIONS

"He has a big head, a lousy temper and a stupid wife who once said 'I do.'"

"Come quick. Rev. Bill, the evangelist has just turned into a block of salt."

"You may be an executive at the office but here you're just another wife."

157

"I'll tell you what's wrong with equal rights if you'll just give me equal time."

"When I said we should separate I was speaking about our province."

"For the last time. The sign does not include the husband you met in our store."

"The high cost of food is no excuse for eating your husband."

"You've been 'laid off,' not 'laid out.'"

"I thought you said *your* mother was paying a visit."

"Let's get some fresh air in here. Close the window."

"This is what I call a steal. By the way, are you a handyman?"

"Get me 'That's Incredible.'"

"You're wasting your time. I'm a married man."

"You still say I have a lot to be thankful for?"

"Ever since Lady Di refused to obey Charles I can't get her to do a damn thing."

"I'm on a diet!"

"Let's make a deal. You stop keeping up with me and I'll stop keeping up with you."

"Obey!
Won't!
Obey!
Won't!"

"He refuses to give me a divorce, isn't that mental cruelty?"

166

"Hey, Mabel, come quick. The Loveboat just hit an iceberg."

"Okay, okay. This year *you* get to decorate the tree."

"Did you order a test-tube baby, Harold?"

"There, you see. In spite of what you told the cops, I didn't shoot J.R."

WHAT'S UP, BILL?

— DON'T TELL ME — YOUR TEAM LOST, RIGHT?

AFTER 60 YEARS OF MARRIAGE DON'T EVER TRY TO HIDE ANYTHING FROM ME, MY LOVE

WE WIN 10-0

WICKS

DO YOU HAVE A SECRET AS TO WHY YOU AND MRS. TRAVIS HAVE REMAINED HAPPILY MARRIED SO LONG?

WE CERTAINLY DO

I'M THE ONE THAT MAKES ALL THE BIG DECISIONS

LIKE WHAT?

LIKE MAVIS SAYS WHEN WE EAT, WHEN WE GO TO BED AND HOW WE SPEND OUR DAY

I SAY WHETHER TRUDEAU SHOULD RETIRE, SHOULD JOE CONTINUE TO LEAD, DOES REAGANOMICS WORK...

HOW WAS YOUR DAY DEAR

LOUSY— ROXANNE REFUSED TO BRING ME COFFEE

SAID SHE'S A SECRETARY, NOT A SERVANT AND THAT IF I WANTED COFFEE I SHOULD MAKE IT MYSELF

DID YOU TELL HER I DO IT ALL THE TIME?

I DID AND SHE SAID THAT'S DIFFERENT— YOU'RE A WIFE

WICKS

THE NEW T.V. FALL SCHEDULE SHOULD REALLY SELL T.V. SETS

I KNOW— I'M READY TO SELL OURS

WICKS

"Don't yell at me! It's not my fault you picked a loser."

"I think we've got money left over. What do you want for Christmas?"

"I said the U.S. is $200 billion in the hole, not us."

"He treats me like a wife."

"And while you're thanking God, don't forget the cook."

"Okay, okay. So you're 50 and can kick as high as Shirley MacLaine. Now can I have my supper?"

"Yes, yes, darling. Of course I'll give you a divorce."

"Did you order a hit team?"

"It's your own fault. You know you become allergic to mistletoe if you stand under it too long."

"I'm sick of your feminist attitudes. I'm going home to mother."

"Men have rights too, you know."

"You can't lay me off. I quit!"

"It's finally happened. I can't remember whether I'm retired or unemployed."

"Today is Thanksgiving so I'll thank you to shut up while I'm reading."

MATERNITY

"Look children, it's Daddy making a guest appearance."

"I suggested collective bargaining but he insisted. 'Thou shalt not commit adultery' stays in."

"It makes you look fat."

"I thought you were going to the beauty parlour."

"Stop bitching. It was you who wanted to take break-dancing lessons."

"You may be an adviser in Nicaragua, but here you're just another husband."

"Give me five minutes' start before you tackle the Easter egg I got you."

"You wanted me to cut back on our food bill so I cut back."

"He can't talk now, he's trying to quit smoking."

"When the Pope starts taking his wife on business trips, I'll take you."

"I don't care what it says. You're not going to Paris on business and that's final."

"Of course it won't fit, stupid. This is a sale."

"This is a heck of a time to be asking for a divorce."

"If you don't want to quit smoking, what do you want to do?"

"It's a good job I came home early. You're missing the Queen."

"He wants an expensive gift for his wife."

"I'd like to adopt a dependant."

"Great news. I almost got a job today."

"And another thing. Where were you when it was time to kiss in the New Year?"

"Don't tell me. You've found a job, right?"

"Henry, why do I feel that we're drifting apart?"

"In addition, if your wife got hit by an atomic missile...Russian, of course..."

"I assure you madam, this has nothing to do with the fact that your husband is a hypochondriac."

"I would have bought you a Valentine card but they were too expensive."

"And don't try to stop me."

"Frankly, Harold, I preferred you when you were smoking."

"So how's the rest of the world?"

"That bridge you once bought is 100 years old today."

"That reminds me. When are you coming off your diet?"

VI

What can I tell you.
Kids are great.
What else is good?
Well, you're near the end of the book.
This is the last section.
If you're still standing in the store reading this, do me a favour.
Laugh a couple of times.
There are others in the store.
Maybe one of them will buy a copy.

**"I don't know why the wolf didn't use a
nuclear device to blow down the house.
Now can I continue?"**

"Okay. So you look like Linda Evans. Now can I have my ball back?"

"And please put the Christmas bills on hold until February."

"Does anyone here speak French?"

"The teachers are still on strike."

"Do you have air conditioning?"

"No thanks, I'm trying to quit."

"Don't be silly. As long as both sides are strong and powerful, there's no way we'll become extinct."

"One day, all this won't be yours."

"Now here's what I want. Better wages, better fringe benefits, better..."

"Sure I know what it is. My dad once had one."

"If we separate from the rest of Canada does that mean I'll be a foreigner?"

"Sure I can loan you a couple of bucks. How does one above prime grab you?"

"You gave me this last Christmas and forgot to show me how to do it."

"How come there are so many of us? Because there are so many of you, that's why."

"I don't get it. Glenn has been a space man – why would he want to be just a president?"

"Why aren't you at home getting packed for your trip?"

Class of '84

"Name?"

"What do you think you're doing?"

"Once upon a time there was a big, bad, peace activist..."

"I just want a credit card."

"You're the best so far but I have one more to see. The boss's son."

"For the last time, no, you cannot claim her as a dependant."

"It's not fair. I was aborted from the game last week."

"For Pete's sake, Harold, stop that. Have you seen our heating bill for this month?"

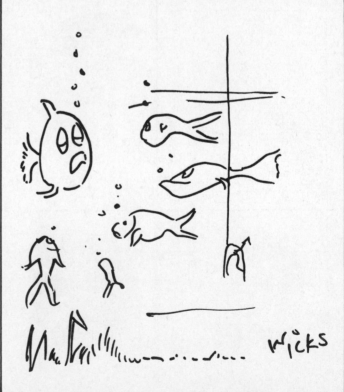

"It's been proposed and seconded. No more bait biting until they act on acid rain."

"My Dad has been laid off and said you're not coming this year. How come?"

"Change or no change. You're not coming with me and that's final."

"Tell me again. Why are you returning your son's chemistry set?"

"Ho, ho, ho."

"Just answer the charge. Are you guilty or not guilty of breaking and entering."

"You're right. It is a McDonald's."

"Keep getting marks like this and you'll end up in politics."

"Negotiations with Santa broke down today, making the possibility of a strike highly likely."

"I knew there was something wrong when it showed we had an opening for a youth."

"He claims he was kicked by a reindeer."

"You've missed someone."

"New boots, sutures, a new bolt..."

"And so, Sleeping Beauty, sick of his playing around, left Prince Charming and lived happily ever after."

"Ooops. Guess who I forgot?"

"I'm starting you off at the top, son. We're laying off at the bottom."

"Mom, Dad just said a naughty word."

"Isn't it wonderful, dear? Our little baby's first day of unemployment."

"Here comes another human. Shall we eat him now or wait for him to destroy himself?"

"Why doesn't he learn something worthwhile. Like the guitar or lobbying?"

"It must be some form of government. You can tell by the direction they're travelling."

"Actually, it was my son who noticed something was wrong when he jumped on it to ride."

"Daddy has just found out that he's the same age as Julio Iglesias."

"Okay, so it's not porridge. Have you seen the price of porridge lately?"

"I see a short, fat, jolly man in a red suit."

"And I'm telling you that you can't taste acid rain."

"You're in luck. We've got one left."

"There's a guy outside pretending to be you."

"In the beginning, there was peace."

"I'm skipping buying a present for
Father's Day this year. Any objections?"

"How do we know that this reference
from Snow White is genuine?"

"What do you mean 'a lot of little people'
made them for you?"

"Now this is a tough word since you don't
hear it too often. Em...ploy...ed."

"I'll prove to you there's no acid rain in your water. Here Frank, drink this."

"As near as I could find out they're an endangered species."

"Hey, Mom and Dad. I've finally found a job."

"Congratulations. You've got another mouth to feed."

"And come straight home."

"They've gone to see E.T."

"I'm waiting for the day that they can transplant legs."

"It's Cyndi Lauper."

218

"It's time we had a chat about the facts of life. This is a bill."

"How do you expect to become prime minister if you keep fidgeting during rest period?"

"Someday, son, all this will be yours."

"I don't care how advanced your generation is, you're not having the keys to the car and that's final."

"How do you expect to get a blessing if you don't wave your flag?"

"Just stay where you are and blow me a kiss."

"You hold it steady while I put the star on top."

"Then the young lad left school and found a job."

"If you don't learn how to read, how are you going to understand the 'help wanted' columns?"

"Gee, I'm sorry. We don't have any work for students. Have you tried Pluto?"

"Which ones are pieces of our garbage and which are the stars?"

"Past the small bush on the right, left at the palm tree and then ask again."

"It just so happens, I don't care what you believe in."

"I was working in a nuclear plant and one day there was a leak."

"Threatening to strike is hardly what we expect from our Santa."

"Guess who's expecting twins in September?"

"Are you sure you don't want an appliance? They're on special."

"Come quick, sir. I think Santa's been drinking."

"We're building bigger and better bombs so that you won't have to build bigger and better bombs."

"The job's been filled. However, if you don't mind waiting..."

"You're lucky. Have you any idea how many students are without a summer job?"

"It's from his English teacher. He says, 'He ain't doing no good.'"

"Look, Dad, a mirage."

"I have an unexpected fiscal imbalance."